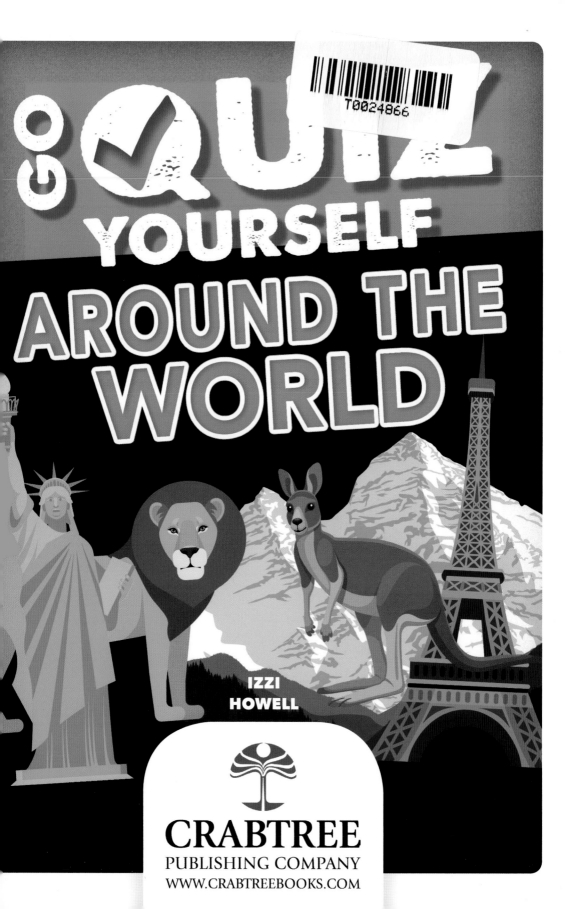

GO QUIZ YOURSELF AROUND THE WORLD

IZZI HOWELL

CRABTREE
PUBLISHING COMPANY
WWW.CRABTREEBOOKS.COM

CRABTREE
PUBLISHING COMPANY
WWW.CRABTREEBOOKS.COM

Author: Izzi Howell
Editorial director: Kathy Middleton
Series editor: Izzi Howell
Editor: Crystal Sikkens
Proofreader: Wendy Scavuzzo
Series design: Rocket Design (East Anglia) Ltd
Prepress technician: Katherine Berti
Print coordinator: Katherine Berti

Every effort has been made to clear copyright.
Should there be any inadvertent omission,
please apply to the publisher for rectification.

The website addresses (URLs) included in this book were
valid at the time of going to press. However, it is possible that
contents or addresses may have changed since the publication
of this book. No responsibility for any such changes can be
accepted by either the author or the publisher.

All facts and statistics were correct at the time of press.

Picture acknowledgements: Getty: PytyCzech 7t, moonery 27, JTSorrell 37c; Peter Bull: 32–33c; Techtype: 36t; Shutterstock: Top Vector Studio, Daria Riabets, SaveJungle, Spreadthesign and Merfin cover and title page, Lidiia Koval 4, Sudowoodo 5t, Reenya 5b, okili77 6, 8, 12, 14, 18 and 20, Malchev, Zvereva Yana, narak0rn, K.Kyere and LineTale 6–7b, Spreadthesign, Valeri Hadeev and SaveJungle 7t, 77Ivan 7cl, Maquiladora 7cr, olegtoka nimograf, Sky Designs, Red monkey and Chalintra.B 8–9b, Olleg 9t, Sentavio, Maquiladora, Shanvood, SaveJungle and Christiane Franke 9c, reuse from pages 6–9 10–11, Sentavio, Tomacco, VectoRaith and imdproduction 12–13b, Antikwar 13t, SaveJungle, Rhoeo, Maquiladora, Daria Riabets and Professional Bat 13c, Bluehousestudio, Sentavio, Chalintra.B, Alexander Ryabintsev and Red monkey 14–15b, Jesus Sanz 15t, Hennadii H, Pogorelova Olga, Giraffarte and Maria Siubar 15c, reuse from pages 12–15 16–17, Infinity Eternity, Sentavio, studioworkstock and SaveJungle 18–19b, Faya Francevna 19t, AnnstasAg, Gaidamashchuk, Nadya_Art, A7880S, iana kauri, HappyPictures and Maquiladora 19c, Nadya_Art, Dimec, A7880S and Genesis Parra 20–21b, saiko3p 21t, A7880S, Rhoeo, Eno Boy and GoodStudio 21c, reuse from pages 18–21 22–23, DidGason 24t, LANTERIA 24b, matrioshka 25t, A7880S 25b, Teresa Prokhoryan 26t, Peter Hermes Furian 26b, Sunnydream, Chonnanit, Rvector, Shanvood and KittyVector 27, reuse from pages 24–27 28–29, Yusiki 30, Midorie 31t, Natali Snailcat 31b, SaveJungle, Elegant Solution and joilaird 32, Lidiia, SaveJungle, Zvereva Yana, ActiveLines and Tikofff1 33, reuse from pages 30–33 34–35, Kseniya Art 36b, Arsgera 37t, Oceloti 37b, Zvereva Yana 38t, rudvi 38c, passengerz 38b, ActiveLines 38–39, Mascha Tace, Kaewta and Nadya_Art 39, reuse from pages 36–39 40–41, all_is_magic 42t, Studio Ayutaka 42c, whyt 42b, lady-luck 43t, Maryna Yakovchuk 43c, Blan-k 43b, Lidiia Koval 45, reuse from book 46–47. All design elements from Shutterstock.

Library and Archives Canada Cataloguing in Publication

Title: Go quiz yourself around the world / Izzi Howell.
Other titles: Around the world
Names: Howell, Izzi, author.
Description: Series statement: Go quiz yourself | Includes index.
Identifiers: Canadiana (print) 20200358294 |
  Canadiana (ebook) 20200358383 |
  ISBN 9781427128713 (hardcover) |
  ISBN 9781427128775 (softcover) |
  ISBN 9781427128836 (HTML)
Subjects: LCSH: Geography–Juvenile literature. |
  LCSH: Geography–Problems, exercises, etc.–Juvenile
  literature. | LCSH: Social sciences–Juvenile literature. |
  LCSH: Social sciences–Problems, exercises, etc.–
  Juvenile literature.
Classification: LCC G133 .H69 2021 | DDC j910–dc23

Library of Congress Cataloging-in-Publication Data

Names: Howell, Izzi, author.
Title: Go quiz yourself around the world / Izzi Howell.
Other titles: Around the world
Description: New York : Crabtree Publishing Company, 2021.
  | Series: Go quiz yourself | At head of title: Go quiz yourself. |
  Audience: Ages 9-14 years+ | Audience: Grades 4-6 | Summary:
  "Read about the things in our incredible world-landmarks,
  habitats and wildlife from the seven continents, dry deserts, huge
  oceans, mighty mountains, and much more. Then see if you can
  answer questions, such as: Which country is made up of over
  6,000 islands? How many languages are spoken on Earth? What
  is the deadliest large land animal?"-- Provided by publisher.
Identifiers: LCCN 2020046063 (print) |
  LCCN 2020046064 (ebook) |
  ISBN 9781427128713 (Hardcover) |
  ISBN 9781427128775 (Paperback) |
  ISBN 9781427128836 (eBook)
Subjects: LCSH: Geography--Juvenile literature. | Geography--
  Problems, exercises, etc.--Juvenile literature. | Physical geograph
  -Juvenile literature. | Social sciences--Juvenile literature. | Social
  sciences--Problems, exercises, etc.--Juvenile literature.
Classification: LCC G133 .H68 2021 (print) | LCC G133 (ebook) |
  DDC 910--dc23
LC record available at https://lccn.loc.gov/2020046063
LC ebook record available at https://lccn.loc.gov/2020046064

Crabtree Publishing Company
www.crabtreebooks.com   1-800-387-7650
Published by Crabtree Publishing Company in 2021

First published in Great Britain in 2020 by Wayland
Copyright ©Hodder and Stoughton Limited, 2020

**Published
in Canada
Crabtree Publishing**
616 Welland Ave.
St. Catharines, Ontario
L2M 5V6

**Published in
the United States
Crabtree Publishing**
347 Fifth Ave
Suite 1402-145
New York, NY 10016

Printed in the U.S.A./122020/CG20201014

CONTENTS

HOW TO USE THIS BOOK

This book is packed full of amazing facts and statistics. When you've finished reading a section, test yourself with questions on the following pages. Check your answers on pages 44–45 and see if you're a quizmaster or if you need to quiz it again! When you've finished, test your friends and family to find out who's the ultimate quiz champion!

OUR WORLD

Planet Earth is our home. It is the only known place in the universe that contains life. People around the world in different countries have a wide range of cultures, identities, languages, and religions.

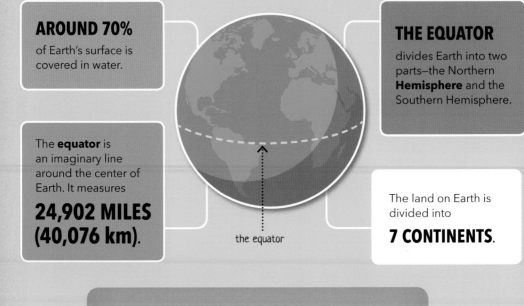

AROUND 70%
of Earth's surface is covered in water.

THE EQUATOR
divides Earth into two parts—the Northern **Hemisphere** and the Southern Hemisphere.

The **equator** is an imaginary line around the center of Earth. It measures
24,902 MILES (40,076 km).

the equator

The land on Earth is divided into
7 CONTINENTS.

GROWING NUMBERS In 10,000 BCE, the world population was 4 million.

WORLD POPULATION

The world population is 7.5 billion and growing. For most of human history, the population on Earth was low. However, as health care, food production, and cleanliness improved, the population increased dramatically. If the world's population continues to grow in this way, we won't have enough resources to go around.

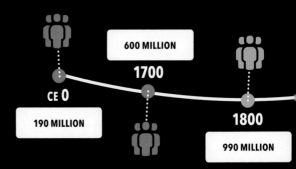

CE 0

190 MILLION

600 MILLION

1700

1800

990 MILLION

COUNTRIES

According to the United Nations, there are 193 countries on Earth.
The newest country is South Sudan, which became independent in 2011.
What is considered a country is a political issue. Some areas, such as
Kosovo, would like to become their own country, but are not able to yet.

PEOPLE OF THE WORLD

The world is a **diverse** place, full of different habitats, animals,
people, cultures, and languages. It is important to learn about
other people around the world and respect their ways of life.

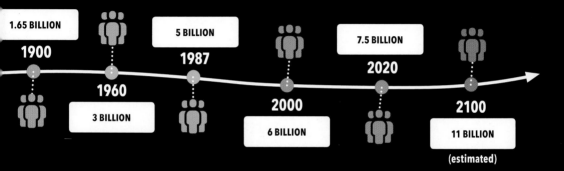

1.65 BILLION
1900

3 BILLION
1960

5 BILLION
1987

6 BILLION
2000

7.5 BILLION
2020

11 BILLION
(estimated)
2100

AFRICA

The continent **of Africa covers about one-fifth of the land on Earth. It stretches for 4,971 miles (8,000 km) from north to south, from the Mediterranean coast down to the bottom of South Africa.**

Number of countries: **54**

Size: **11,723,992 square miles (30,365,000 square km)**

Population: **1.35 billion**

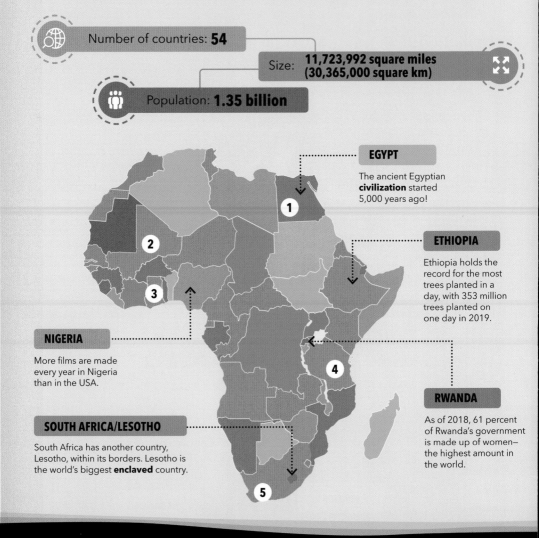

EGYPT

The ancient Egyptian **civilization** started 5,000 years ago!

ETHIOPIA

Ethiopia holds the record for the most trees planted in a day, with 353 million trees planted on one day in 2019.

NIGERIA

More films are made every year in Nigeria than in the USA.

RWANDA

As of 2018, 61 percent of Rwanda's government is made up of women— the highest amount in the world.

SOUTH AFRICA/LESOTHO

South Africa has another country, Lesotho, within its borders. Lesotho is the world's biggest **enclaved** country.

AFRICAN LANDMARKS

1 **Pyramids in Giza, Egypt**

2 **Great Mosque of Djenné, Mali**

THE EQUATOR

The equator runs through the center of the continent, going through seven African countries. The area around the equator has a tropical, wet **climate** with regions of rain forest. To the north and the south of the equator are grasslands, known as savanna. Beyond the grasslands are dry deserts, such as the Sahara and the Kalahari.

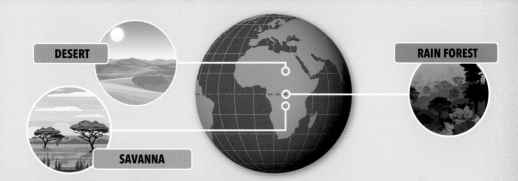

DESERT

RAIN FOREST

SAVANNA

EARLY HUMANS

Scientists believe that humans (*Homo sapiens*) first evolved in Africa around 315,000 years ago.

Archaeologists have found many remains of humans and early human **ancestors** in East Africa.

They studied these bones to understand how humans evolved.

The first humans migrated out of Africa and traveled across the world.

MEGA BEASTS

Africa is home to the world's tallest animal, the giraffe, and the largest land animal, the African bush elephant. One of the deadliest land animals, the hippopotamus, is also found in Africa. Hippopotamuses are very aggressive and have sharp teeth.

hippopotamus

giraffe

African bush elephant

EUROPE

Europe is the second-smallest continent. It is connected by land to Asia in the east. Europe stretches from Iceland and Scandinavia in the north to Greece, Italy, and Spain in the south.

Number of countries: **50***

*(3 of which also have land in Asia)

Size: **3,861,022 square miles (10 million square km)**

Population: **748 million**

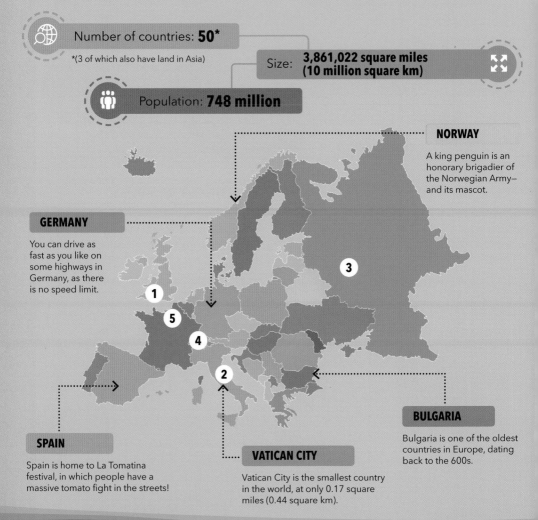

NORWAY

A king penguin is an honorary brigadier of the Norwegian Army— and its mascot.

GERMANY

You can drive as fast as you like on some highways in Germany, as there is no speed limit.

BULGARIA

Bulgaria is one of the oldest countries in Europe, dating back to the 600s.

SPAIN

Spain is home to La Tomatina festival, in which people have a massive tomato fight in the streets!

VATICAN CITY

Vatican City is the smallest country in the world, at only 0.17 square miles (0.44 square km).

EUROPEAN LANDMARKS

THE EUROPEAN UNION

Twenty-seven European countries are members of the European Union (EU). The EU was created to make it easier for European countries to trade with each other. Citizens of EU countries can move freely between any countries in the EU. Many EU countries use the same currency—the Euro.

the flag of the European Union

EUROPEAN WILDLIFE

Europe and Asia are connected, so many animals live on both continents since they can move freely back and forth. However, there are some animals that are unique to Europe.

Iberian lynx

pine marten

red kite

European badger

ANCIENT CIVILIZATIONS

Europe was home to two massive ancient civilizations—ancient Greece and ancient Rome. The ancient Greeks introduced the world to democracy, the Olympic Games, and philosophy. The ancient Romans built great buildings and roads, and developed the alphabet that is used in English and many other languages around the world.

ancient Greek Acropolis ·········> in Athens, Greece

3 St Basil's Cathedral, Russia

4 Matterhorn,

5 Eiffel Tower, France

GO QUIZ YOURSELF!

1 How much of Earth's surface is covered in water?

2 How many continents are there on Earth?

3 What is the newest country?

4 What was the world population in 10,000 BCE?

5 What was the world population in 2020?

6 How many countries are there in Africa?

7 Which country is found within the borders of South Africa?

8 In which African country is Mount Kilimanjaro?

9 What is the climate like around the equator in Africa?

10 When did humans (*Homo sapiens*) first evolve in Africa?

11 Which African animal is the largest land animal?

12 Which continent is Europe connected to?

13 How large is Europe?

14 Which European country is the smallest country in the world?

15 In which European country is the Colosseum found?

16 What is the shared currency of many EU countries?

17 Which ancient civilization introduced democracy, philosophy, and the Olympic Games to the world?

ASIA

Asia is the largest continent with the highest population. It occupies around one-third of all land on Earth. Asia stretches from Turkey in the west to Indonesia and Japan in the east.

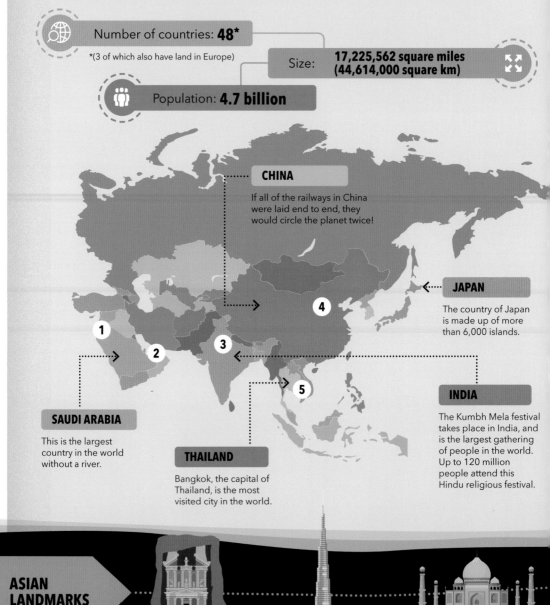

Number of countries: **48***

*(3 of which also have land in Europe)

Size: **17,225,562 square miles (44,614,000 square km)**

Population: **4.7 billion**

CHINA

If all of the railways in China were laid end to end, they would circle the planet twice!

JAPAN

The country of Japan is made up of more than 6,000 islands.

1

2

3

4

5

SAUDI ARABIA

This is the largest country in the world without a river.

THAILAND

Bangkok, the capital of Thailand, is the most visited city in the world.

INDIA

The Kumbh Mela festival takes place in India, and is the largest gathering of people in the world. Up to 120 million people attend this Hindu religious festival.

ASIAN LANDMARKS

PEOPLE AND POPULATION

China and India, two of the largest countries in the world by population, are located in Asia. Both are home to more than 1 billion people. Russia, the largest country in the world by size, is also mainly located in Asia, although some of its territory is also in Europe. Some of the smaller Asian countries by size, such as Singapore and Bangladesh, also have large populations, resulting in a high **population density**.

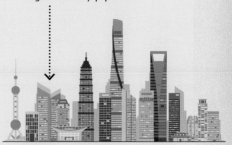

Shanghai is one of China's largest cities by population.

Mount Everest

HIGHS AND LOWS

The highest and lowest points on Earth are in Asia. The highest point is Mount Everest in the Himalayas, reaching 29,035 feet (8,850 m) above sea level. The lowest point on land is the Dead Sea, found in Israel and Jordan, which measures 1,411 feet (430 m) below sea level.

WILDLIFE

There are many different habitats in Asia, from the high mountains of the Himalayas to the rain forests of Southeast Asia, and grassy plains of China. This has led to a diverse range of animal life, with many species that can only be found in Asia.

SNOW LEOPARD
central Asia

ORANGUTAN
islands of Sumatra and Borneo

TIGER
parts of India, China, Russia, and Southeast Asia

GIANT PANDA
China

KING COBRA
India and Southeast Asia

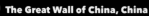

4 **The Great Wall of China, China**

5 **Angkor Wat, Cambodia**

OCEANIA

Oceania is made up of the islands of Australia, New Zealand, and over 10,000 other islands in the Pacific Ocean, such as Fiji, Tahiti, and Samoa. Australia is the largest and most-populated country in Oceania.

Number of countries: **14**

Size: **3,291,903 square miles (8,525,989 square km)**

Population: **42.8 million**

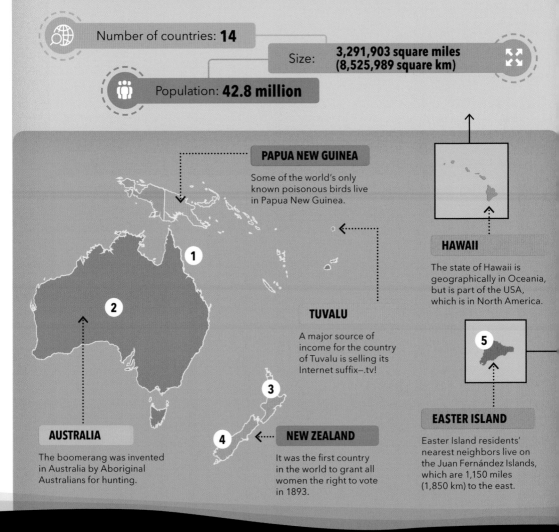

PAPUA NEW GUINEA

Some of the world's only known poisonous birds live in Papua New Guinea.

HAWAII

The state of Hawaii is geographically in Oceania, but is part of the USA, which is in North America.

TUVALU

A major source of income for the country of Tuvalu is selling its Internet suffix–.tv!

EASTER ISLAND

Easter Island residents' nearest neighbors live on the Juan Fernández Islands, which are 1,150 miles (1,850 km) to the east.

AUSTRALIA

The boomerang was invented in Australia by Aboriginal Australians for hunting.

NEW ZEALAND

It was the first country in the world to grant all women the right to vote in 1893.

OCEANIA LANDMARKS

 1 Great Barrier Reef, Australia

 2 Uluru, Australia

CITIES

The top-ten largest cities in Oceania are all in Australia and New Zealand. Sydney, Australia, is the largest, with more than 5.2 million people. The smaller, remote islands in Oceania tend to have smaller populations. People live in towns and villages, where the main industries are tourism and farming.

Sydney

PEOPLE

Before European people invaded countries in Oceania, there were many **Indigenous** groups of people across the islands, such as the Māori in New Zealand and Aboriginal Australians. After the European invasion, a huge number of Indigenous peoples were wiped out by disease. Land was stolen from them and they were forced to change their culture. Although people try to protect and celebrate these cultures today, Indigenous peoples still face prejudice.

MARSUPIALS AND MONOTREMES

Oceania is home to a group of **mammals** called marsupials. These animals give birth to their young before they are fully developed. Marsupial young attach themselves to their mother, sometimes in a pouch, and drink her milk while they finish developing. It is also home to another unusual group of mammals called monotremes. These mammals lay eggs instead of giving birth to live young.

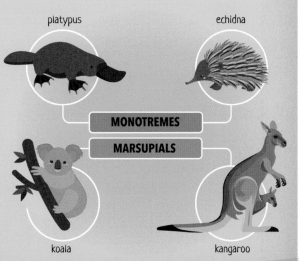

platypus

echidna

MONOTREMES

MARSUPIALS

koala

kangaroo

GO QUIZ YOURSELF!

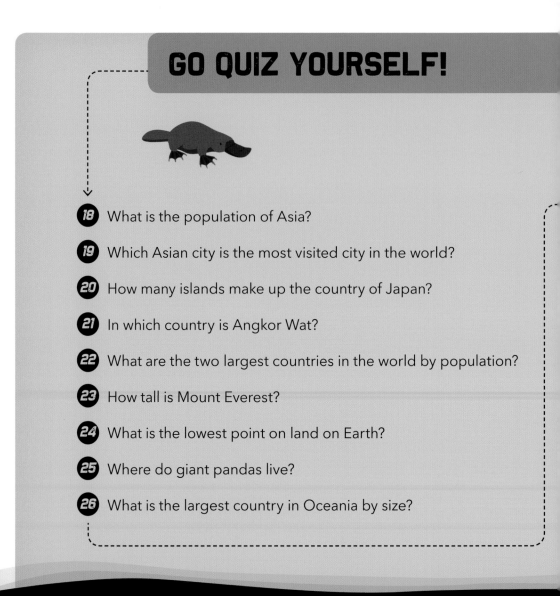

18 What is the population of Asia?

19 Which Asian city is the most visited city in the world?

20 How many islands make up the country of Japan?

21 In which country is Angkor Wat?

22 What are the two largest countries in the world by population?

23 How tall is Mount Everest?

24 What is the lowest point on land on Earth?

25 Where do giant pandas live?

26 What is the largest country in Oceania by size?

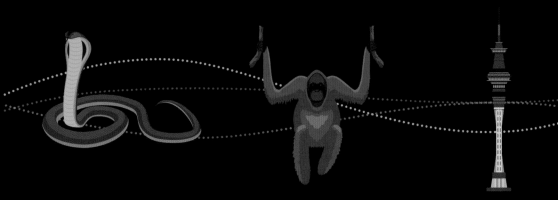

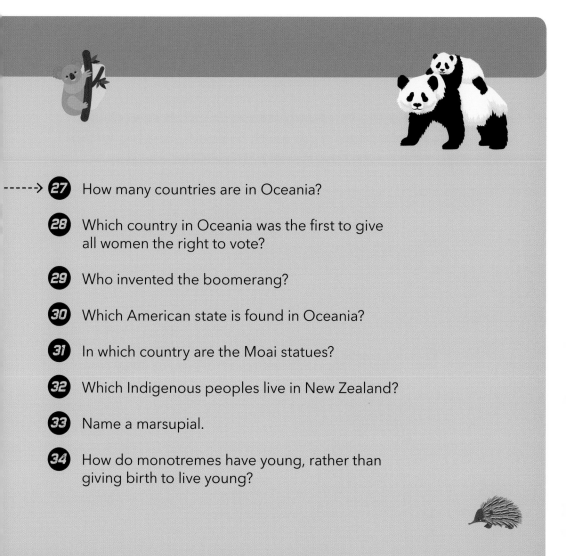

27 How many countries are in Oceania?

28 Which country in Oceania was the first to give all women the right to vote?

29 Who invented the boomerang?

30 Which American state is found in Oceania?

31 In which country are the Moai statues?

32 Which Indigenous peoples live in New Zealand?

33 Name a marsupial.

34 How do monotremes have young, rather than giving birth to live young?

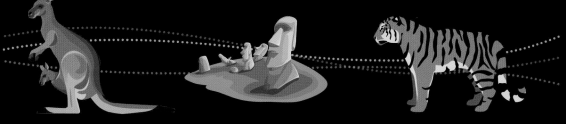

NORTH AMERICA

North America is the third-largest continent. It stretches for 4,971 miles (8,000 km) from north to south, coming within 497 miles (800 km) of the North Pole and the equator.

Number of countries: **23**

Size: **9,355,255 square miles (24,230,000 square km)**

Population: **369 million**

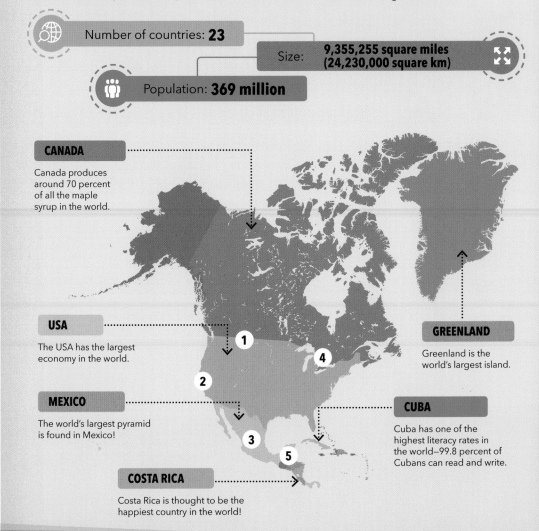

CANADA

Canada produces around 70 percent of all the maple syrup in the world.

USA

The USA has the largest economy in the world.

MEXICO

The world's largest pyramid is found in Mexico!

COSTA RICA

Costa Rica is thought to be the happiest country in the world!

GREENLAND

Greenland is the world's largest island.

CUBA

Cuba has one of the highest literacy rates in the world—99.8 percent of Cubans can read and write.

NORTH AMERICAN LANDMARKS

CITIES

Some of the largest cities on Earth are found in North America. Mexico City, the capital of Mexico, is the largest city in North America. In the USA, many people live in the huge cities of New York and Los Angeles.

New York

NORTH TO SOUTH

The north of the continent is close to the North Pole. This area has cold temperatures and ice and snow. As you move south, the most common habitats are forests and grassland (known as prairies). There are also areas of desert. Central America and the Caribbean islands have a tropical climate with rain forests.

N

caribou

POLAR REGION

polar bear

beaver

FORESTS

moose

bison

PRAIRIES

coyote

gila monster

DESERTS

scorpion

hummingbird

RAIN FORESTS

sloth

S

3 Pyramid of the Sun, Mexico

4 CN Tower, Canada

5 Tikal, Guatemala

19

SOUTH AMERICA

This continent is located to the south of North America. The two continents are connected by a land bridge that is just 51 miles (82 km) wide in some places. Apart from Antarctica, South America is the continent that reaches farthest south.

Number of countries: **12**

Size: **6,878,024 square miles (17,814,000 square km)**

Population: **431 million**

VENEZUELA

Angel Falls, the world's highest uninterrupted waterfall, is in Venezuela.

ISTHMUS OF PANAMA

This land bridge connects South America to North America, and it is the location of the country of Panama.

ECUADOR

The closest place on Earth to space, Mount Chimborazo, is found in Ecuador. This is because Earth bulges around the equator, so the land is higher here.

BRAZIL

The world's largest carnival takes place in Rio de Janeiro, Brazil. It attracts around 2 million visitors!

PERU

There are more than 6,000 different species of plants in 0.4 square miles (1 square km) of Peruvian rain forest.

CHILE

The oldest mummies in the world were made in Chile in around 5,000 B.C.E., 2,000 years before the ancient Egyptians!

SOUTH AMERICAN LANDMARKS

1 Nazca Lines, Peru

2 Christ the Redeemer, Brazil

HABITATS

There are many different habitats across South America, including tropical rain forests, such as the Amazon, grasslands, known as pampas, and the high mountainous habitat on the Andes Mountains. It is so cold in the south part of the continent that there are **glaciers** and penguins.

THE AMAZON RAIN FOREST

The Amazon rain forest covers around 2.3 million square miles (6 million square km) of South America in the **river basin** of the Amazon River. It is split between Brazil, Peru, Colombia, and other surrounding countries. It is the most biodiverse area on Earth, with millions of species of plants, insects, birds, fish, and mammals. Many species in the Amazon are yet to be discovered by scientists.

🏛 MACHU PICCHU

The remains of the Incan city of Machu Picchu are located in Peru.

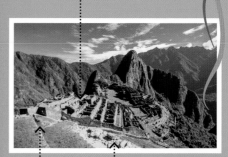

The city is built at a height of 7,710 feet (2,350 m) in the Andes Mountains.

The Inca had a massive **empire** along the west coast of South America in the 1400s and 1500s.

GREEN ANACONDA
near to water in tropical areas

VICUÑA
mountains

ELECTRIC EEL
freshwater around the Amazon River and the Orinoco River

TOUCAN
forests

Native animals

There are many different native **species across South America, in each of its** diverse habitats. Many of **these species can't be found anywhere else in the world.**

JAGUAR
rain forests, wetlands, and grasslands

GO QUIZ YOURSELF!

35 What is the population of North America?

36 Which North American country produces 70 percent of the world's maple syrup?

37 In which North American country is the world's largest pyramid?

38 Which North American country is thought to be the happiest country in the world?

39 In which country is the Golden Gate Bridge?

40 What is the largest city in North America?

41 What is the climate like in the north of North America?

42 Name an animal that lives on the prairies of North America.

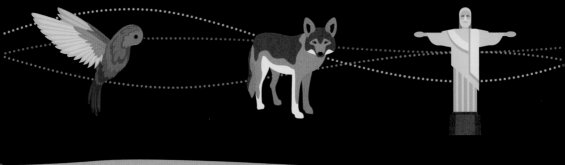

43 How wide is the narrowest point on the Isthmus of Panama— the land bridge between North and South America?

44 How many people attend the world's largest carnival in Rio de Janeiro, Brazil?

45 What is the name of the highest uninterrupted waterfall, which is found in Venezuela?

46 In which country is the statue of Christ the Redeemer?

47 What are the pampas?

48 How large is the Amazon rain forest?

49 Which South American civilization built the city of Machu Picchu?

50 How high is the city of Machu Picchu?

51 In which areas do green anacondas live?

ANTARCTICA

**The continent of Antarctica lies around the South Pole.
It is almost entirely covered with ice.**

Number of countries: **0**

Size: **5,482,651 square miles
(14,200,000 square km)**

Population: **0 permanent residents**

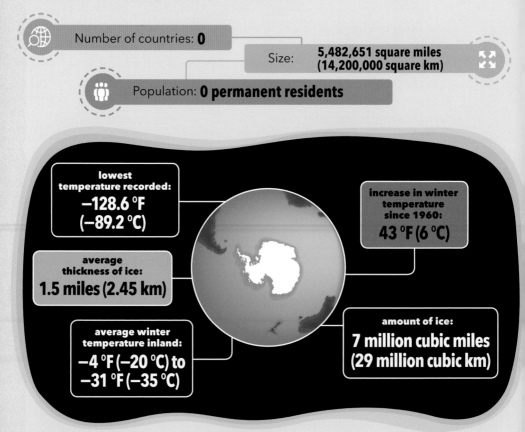

**lowest
temperature recorded:
−128.6 °F
(−89.2 °C)**

**increase in winter
temperature
since 1960:
43 °F (6 °C)**

**average
thickness of ice:
1.5 miles (2.45 km)**

**average winter
temperature inland:
−4 °F (−20 °C) to
−31 °F (−35 °C)**

**amount of ice:
7 million cubic miles
(29 million cubic km)**

ICE AND LAND

Unlike the North Pole, there is land under the ice of Antarctica. This
is why it is considered a continent. Some of this ice also extends out
over the ocean, creating an ice shelf. A long chain of mountains runs
through the center of Antarctica. To the east, there is a high **plateau**
and to the west are islands, which are hidden by the ice.

WHO'S IN CHARGE?

Antarctica does not belong to any country. In 1959, many countries signed a **treaty** agreeing that Antarctica should be made an area of scientific research for all nations. No armies, weapons, or military bases are allowed. Drilling for oil on Antarctica is also forbidden.

SCIENTIFIC RESEARCH

Many different types of scientific research are carried out on Antarctica. Scientists live and work at research stations, usually just for part of the year. They study the climate, **geology**, and wildlife of Antarctica. It is also a great location to study space, as there is little light or air pollution to block the view of the stars.

PLANTS AND ANIMALS

There aren't many plant species on Antarctica, other than lichens. There is a huge amount of life in the seas around Antarctica, including fish, whales, and seals. A few species, such as penguins, live on the ice.

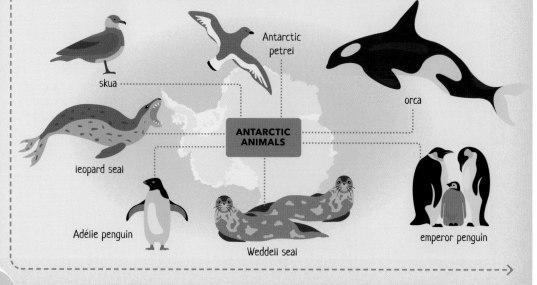

skua

Antarctic petrel

orca

leopard seal

ANTARCTIC ANIMALS

Adélie penguin

Weddell seal

emperor penguin

CULTURE, LANGUAGE, AND RELIGION

People around the world speak different languages, practice different customs, eat different foods, and follow different religions. This is all part of the rich tapestry that makes our planet so special.

● LANGUAGES

Today, just over 7,000 languages are spoken on Earth. Some are used by millions of people, while others are spoken by just a handful. Languages around the world are written in different alphabets and in different directions (left to right, right to left, top to bottom). Many people speak more than one language.

CIAO! SALVE! HEJ! SALUT! SVEIKI! Γεια σας! DZIEŃ DOBRY! MERHABA! ПРИ ¡HOLA! HALLO! 你好! HI! OLÁ! H AHOJ! HELLO! こんにちは SALOM!

MOST SPOKEN FIRST LANGUAGES

1	2	3	4	5
Mandarin Chinese	Spanish	English	Hindi	Arabic

RELIGION

Around 84 percent of people consider themselves to be part of an organized religion. Some religions are more common in certain parts of the world. For example, 99 percent of Hindus and Buddhists live in Asia. Over time, the number of people who follow each religion changes. At the moment, Islam is the fastest-growing religion, followed by Christianity.

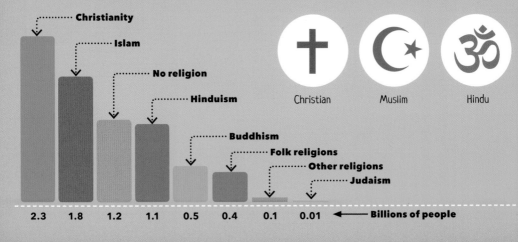

- Christianity
- Islam
- No religion
- Hinduism
- Buddhism
- Folk religions
- Other religions
- Judaism

Christian   Muslim   Hindu

| 2.3 | 1.8 | 1.2 | 1.1 | 0.5 | 0.4 | 0.1 | 0.01 | ◀ Billions of people |

DELICACIES AROUND THE WORLD

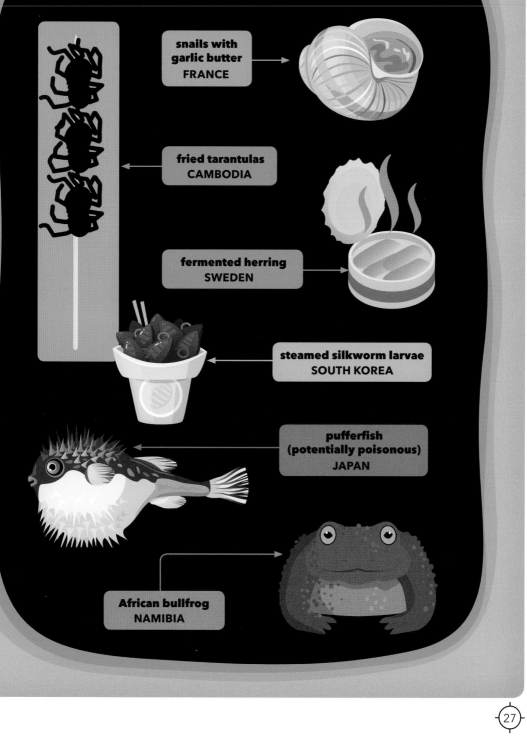

snails with garlic butter
FRANCE

fried tarantulas
CAMBODIA

fermented herring
SWEDEN

steamed silkworm larvae
SOUTH KOREA

**pufferfish
(potentially poisonous)**
JAPAN

African bullfrog
NAMIBIA

GO QUIZ YOURSELF!

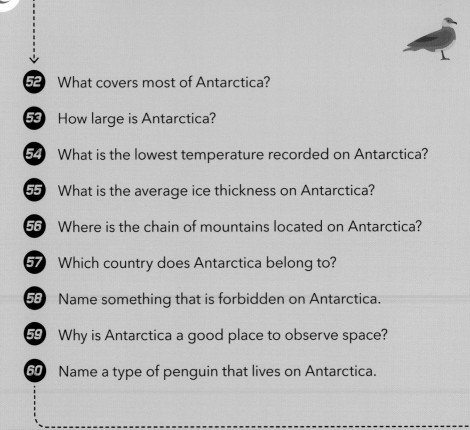

52 What covers most of Antarctica?

53 How large is Antarctica?

54 What is the lowest temperature recorded on Antarctica?

55 What is the average ice thickness on Antarctica?

56 Where is the chain of mountains located on Antarctica?

57 Which country does Antarctica belong to?

58 Name something that is forbidden on Antarctica.

59 Why is Antarctica a good place to observe space?

60 Name a type of penguin that lives on Antarctica.

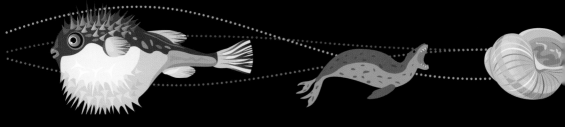

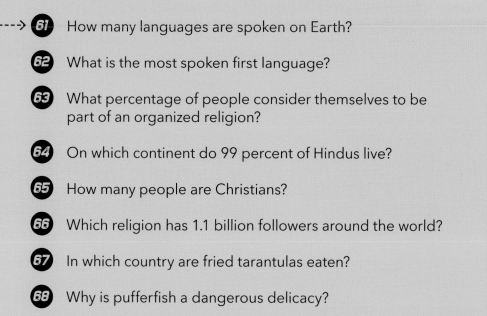

OCEANS

Most of the water on Earth is salt water, which is found in the ocean. We think of Earth's water as five separate oceans, but they are all connected.

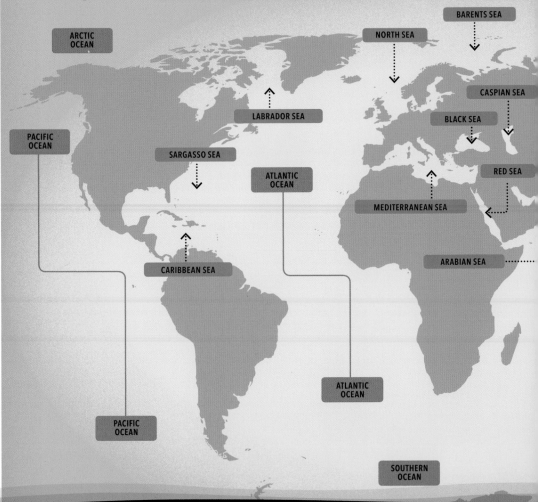

BARENTS SEA

ARCTIC OCEAN

NORTH SEA

CASPIAN SEA

LABRADOR SEA

BLACK SEA

PACIFIC OCEAN

SARGASSO SEA

RED SEA

ATLANTIC OCEAN

MEDITERRANEAN SEA

CARIBBEAN SEA

ARABIAN SEA

ATLANTIC OCEAN

PACIFIC OCEAN

SOUTHERN OCEAN

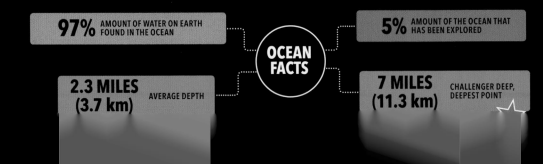

OCEAN FACTS

97% AMOUNT OF WATER ON EARTH FOUND IN THE OCEAN

5% AMOUNT OF THE OCEAN THAT HAS BEEN EXPLORED

2.3 MILES (3.7 km) AVERAGE DEPTH

7 MILES (11.3 km) CHALLENGER DEEP, DEEPEST POINT

SEAS

Seas are smaller areas of the ocean and are often near land. There are many more seas than oceans.

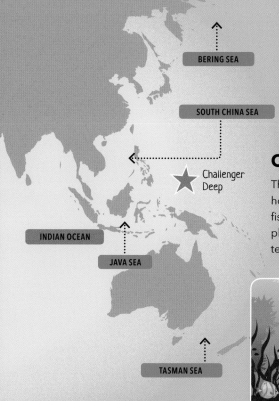

BERING SEA

SOUTH CHINA SEA

Challenger Deep

INDIAN OCEAN

JAVA SEA

TASMAN SEA

≈ SEA OR LAKE?

The Caspian Sea is the largest inland sea—it is completely surrounded by land! Although it sounds like a lake, it's actually a sea, because it contains salt water. In the past, the Caspian Sea was connected to the ocean, but its connection dried up, leaving the sea behind.

OCEAN LIFE

The ocean is the largest habitat on Earth. It is home to millions of different species, including fish, mammals, **invertebrates**, reptiles, and plants. Different animals live in different water temperatures and at different depths.

OCEANS BY SIZE

PACIFIC
62,455,885
SQUARE MILES
(161,760,000
SQUARE KM)

ATLANTIC
32,870,035
SQUARE MILES
(85,133,000
SQUARE KM)

INDIAN
27,243,368
SQUARE MILES
(70,560,000
SQUARE KM)

SOUTHERN
8,478,803
SQUARE MILES
(21,960,000
SQUARE KM)

ARCTIC
6,006,977
SQUARE MILES
(15,558,000
SQUARE KM)

RIVERS

Rivers transform the landscape, providing water to towns and cities and allowing us to move people and goods by ship. These are some of the largest and most important rivers on Earth.

MISSISSIPPI RIVER

★ **Location:** USA (North America)

★ **Length:** 2,340 miles (3,766 km)

★ **Claim to fame:** One of the world's busiest trading routes

AMAZON RIVER

★ **Location:** Brazil, Peru, and Colombia (South America)

★ **Length:** 3,977 miles (6,400 km)

★ **Claim to fame:** The most water discharged by one river. It is estimated to carry one-fifth of all the water that runs across Earth's surface.

Blue Nile

White Nile

NILE RIVER

(Its main tributaries are the White Nile and Blue Nile.)

★ **Location:** Egypt, Sudan, and nine others (Africa)

★ **Length:** 4,132 miles (6,650 km)

★ **Claim to fame:** The longest river in the world

VOLGA RIVER

★ **Location:** Russia (Europe)

★ **Length:** 2,193 miles (3,530 km)

★ **Claim to fame:** Almost half of the population of Russia lives within its basin

YANGTZE RIVER

★ **Location:** China (Asia)

★ **Length:** 3,915 miles (6,300 km)

★ **Claim to fame:** The longest river in Asia and the third-longest in the world

GANGES RIVER

★ **Location:** India (Asia)

★ **Length:** 1,560 miles (2,510 km)

★ **Claim to fame:** The river is **holy** to the Hindu religion

MURRAY RIVER

★ **Location:** Australia (Oceania)

★ **Length:** 1,572 miles (2,530 km)

★ **Claim to fame: Irrigates** more than 70 percent of Australia's farmland

CONGO RIVER

★ **Location:** Democratic Republic of the Congo (Africa)

★ **Length:** 2,920 miles (4,700 km)

★ **Claim to fame:** The world's deepest river

GO QUIZ YOURSELF!

69 How many oceans are there?

70 Which ocean is the farthest north?

71 Name two seas.

72 What is the average depth of the ocean?

73 How deep is Challenger Deep, the deepest point in the ocean?

74 What percentage of the ocean has been explored?

75 What is the largest ocean?

76 What is the largest inland sea?

77 Which river carries one-fifth of all water that runs across Earth's surface?

78 How long is the Amazon River?

79 In which country is the Mississippi River?

80 What is the longest river in the world?

81 What is the longest river in Asia?

82 What is the deepest river in the world?

83 Which river is holy to the Hindu religion?

84 Almost half of the population of Russia lives within the basin of which river?

85 In which country is the Murray River?

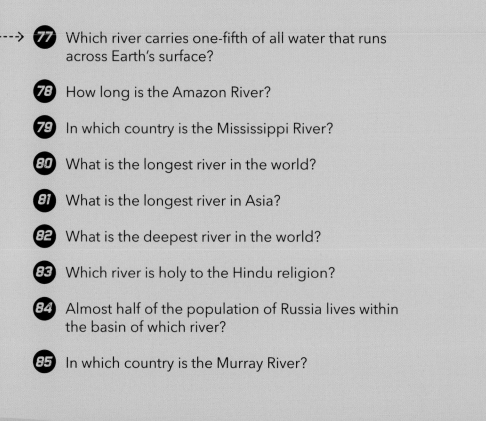

MOUNTAINS

Mountains are tall, rocky areas created by movement of the crust **that covers Earth's surface. Mountains often form in groups, called ranges.**

FORMATION

Earth's crust is divided into sections called tectonic plates. The plates are constantly moving because of movement in the **mantle** beneath them. When tectonic plates collide, the crust between them is pushed upward, forming mountains.

TALL MOUNTAINS

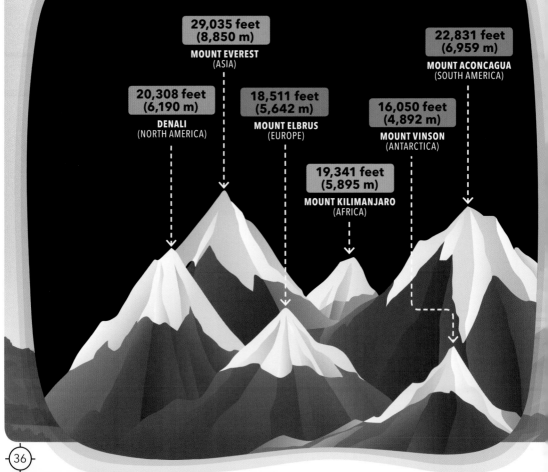

29,035 feet (8,850 m)
MOUNT EVEREST
(ASIA)

22,831 feet (6,959 m)
MOUNT ACONCAGUA
(SOUTH AMERICA)

20,308 feet (6,190 m)
DENALI
(NORTH AMERICA)

18,511 feet (5,642 m)
MOUNT ELBRUS
(EUROPE)

16,050 feet (4,892 m)
MOUNT VINSON
(ANTARCTICA)

19,341 feet (5,895 m)
MOUNT KILIMANJARO
(AFRICA)

OTHER RECORD-BREAKERS

Mount Everest is the tallest mountain on Earth when measured from sea level, but Mauna Kea, Hawaii, USA, is actually taller at more than 32,808 feet (10,000 m). Mauna Kea sits on the seabed, so if you measure from there to its **peak**, it's significantly taller than Everest!

Mount Everest

Mauna Kea

VOLCANOES

Some mountains are volcanoes. Many are active, which means they are currently erupting or may erupt soon. Others are dormant (not expected to erupt soon) or extinct (haven't erupted for at least 10,000 years). During an eruption, hot lava, gas, and ash explode out of a volcano.

VOLCANO FACTS

★ Number of active volcanoes—1,500

★ Number of people who live within the danger zone of an active volcano—350 million

★ Largest volcano—Mauna Loa, Hawaii, USA

★ Most deadly 20th century eruption—Mount Pelée, Martinique, 1902 (29,000 people killed)

DESERTS

Deserts are the driest areas on Earth. They are extreme habitats, with both very high and very low temperatures. They receive almost no rain.

THE LARGEST

The Sahara Desert is the largest desert on Earth. Measuring 3.3 million square miles (8.6 million square km), it's as large as the USA. It is located in Northern Africa.

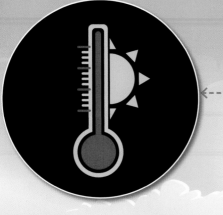

THE HOTTEST

The hottest desert area on Earth is Death Valley. It is located between the Mojave Desert and the Great Basin Desert in Southern California, USA. The hottest temperature ever recorded on Earth was taken there in 1913, reaching a sweltering 134 °F (56.7 °C).

THE COLDEST

Antarctica is considered a desert because it very rarely rains or snows there, so the ice is dry. This makes it the coldest desert on Earth! Some areas of the Arctic are also deserts.

THE LEAST RAIN

The Atacama Desert in Chile, South America, receives almost no rain in some places. In 2018, some parts of the desert received rain for the first time in 500 years. Rain is so unusual there that it disrupted the balance of animals and plants in the area and caused a lot of damage.

DESERT ANIMALS AND PLANTS

Desert animals and plants have adapted to the extreme conditions in different ways.

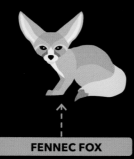

SAGUARO CACTUS

The saguaro cactus has pleats that allow it to expand to fill up with extra water during periods of rain. It stores the water to use during dry periods.

FENNEC FOX

Excess body heat from the fennec fox escapes through its large ears, cooling it down.

EAST AFRICAN ORYX

If water is hard to find, the oryx can survive on moisture from the plants that it eats or by licking dew off rocks.

GO QUIZ YOURSELF!

86 What is a tectonic plate?

87 What is the tallest mountain on Earth, when measured from sea level?

88 On which continent is Denali mountain?

89 What's the tallest mountain in Europe?

90 Which mountain is technically taller than Mount Everest?

91 What does it mean if a volcano is extinct?

92 How many active volcanoes are there on Earth?

93 How many people live within the danger zone of an active volcano?

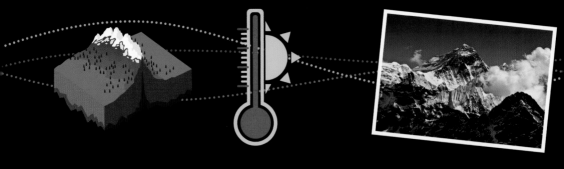

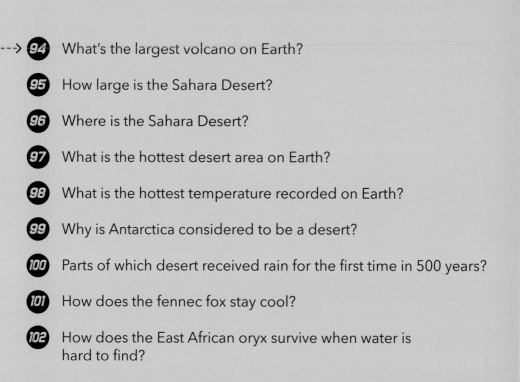

WEIRD AND WONDERFUL PLACES

We often hear about the most famous landmarks and natural areas in a country, but there are a lot of unique and amazing places that don't get the same attention. Some are natural, while others were made by humans.

PINK POND

The water of Lake Hillier, Australia, is a bright pink color! Scientists still aren't entirely sure why the water is pink. It may be because of a reaction between a type of **algae** and the high salt levels in the lake.

CAT COMMUNITY

On the island of Aoshima, Japan, there are more cats than people! For every person on the island, there are six cats. The cats have total freedom to roam around and explore the island.

EASTER ISLAND

This island in the Pacific Ocean is also known as Rapa Nui. It is home to around 900 stone statues of heads and shoulders, known as moai. The moai probably were created to represent the spirits of their ancestors or leaders. Each statue is around 13 feet (4 m) tall and weighs 14 tons (12.7 metric tons)! They were built between the 900s and 1500s and still stand today.

TUNNELS OF BONES

Under the city of Paris, France, is a network of 199 miles (320 km) of tunnels filled with the bones of around 6 million people. In the past, there wasn't enough space above ground to bury these people in cemeteries, so they placed them underground in old quarry tunnels. Later, the skulls and bones were organized in patterns to create a monument to the dead.

MIRROR, MIRROR

The Uyuni Salt Flat in Bolivia, South America, is the world's largest salt flat. A salt flat is created when a lake **evaporates**, leaving behind salt and minerals that cover the ground. This makes the ground white and sometimes reflective, making the Uyuni Salt Flat a giant mirror!

QUIZ TIME!

After you've finished testing yourself, why not use this book to make a quiz to test your friends and family? You could take questions from each section to make different rounds, or mix and match across the book for a general knowledge world quiz. You can even make up your own quiz questions! Use these weird and wonderful places to get you started. For example, **"On which island are there more cats than people?"** or **"Which lake has bright pink water?"**

ANSWERS

1	Around 70 percent	35	369 million
2	7	36	Canada
3	South Sudan	37	Mexico
4	4 million	38	Costa Rica
5	7.5 billion	39	USA
6	54	40	Mexico City
7	Lesotho	41	Cold temperatures with ice and snow
8	Tanzania	42	Bison or coyote (among others)
9	Tropical and wet	43	51 miles (82 km)
10	Around 315,000 years ago	44	2 million people
11	African bush elephant	45	Angel Falls
12	Asia	46	Brazil
13	3,861,022 square miles (10 million square km)	47	Grasslands
		48	Around 2.3 million square miles (6 million square km)
14	Vatican City		
15	Italy	49	The Inca
16	The Euro	50	7,710 feet (2,350 m)
17	Ancient Greece	51	Near to water in tropical areas
18	4.7 billion	52	Ice
19	Bangkok	53	5,482,651 square miles (14,200,000 square km)
20	More than 6,000		
21	Cambodia	54	−128.6 °F (−89.2 °C)
22	China and India	55	1.5 miles (2.4 km)
23	29,035 feet (8,850 m)	56	In the center
24	Dead Sea	57	Antarctica doesn't belong to any country
25	China	58	Armies, weapons, military bases, oil drilling
26	Australia		
27	15	59	Because there is little light or air pollution to block the view of the stars
28	New Zealand		
29	Aboriginal Australians	60	Adélie penguin, emperor penguin
30	Hawaii	61	Just over 7,000
31	Easter Island	62	Mandarin Chinese
32	The Māori	63	Around 84 percent
33	Kangaroo, koala (or wombat)	64	Asia
34	They lay eggs	65	2.3 billion

66	Hinduism	**96**	Northern Africa
67	Cambodia	**97**	Death Valley
68	Because it is potentially poisonous	**98**	134 °F (56.7 °C)
69	Five	**99**	Because it rarely rains or snows there, so the ice is dry
70	The Arctic Ocean	**100**	The Atacama Desert
71	The Arabian Sea, Barents Sea, Bering Sea, Black Sea, Caspian Sea, Caribbean Sea, Java Sea, Labrador Sea, Mediterranean Sea, North Sea, Red Sea, Sargasso Sea, South China Sea, Tasman Sea	**101**	Its body heat escapes through its large ears, helping it to cool down
		102	By getting moisture from plants or by licking dew off rocks
72	2.3 miles (3.7 km)		
73	7 miles (11.3 km)		
74	5 percent		
75	The Pacific Ocean		
76	The Caspian Sea		
77	The Amazon River		
78	3,977 miles (6,400 km)		
79	The USA		
80	The Nile River		
81	The Yangtze River		
82	The Congo River		
83	The Ganges River		
84	The Volga River		
85	Australia		
86	A section of Earth's crust		
87	Mount Everest		
88	North America		
89	Mount Elbrus		
90	Mauna Kea		
91	It hasn't erupted for at least 10,000 years		
92	1,500		
93	350 million		
94	Mauna Loa		
95	3.3 million square miles (8.6 million square km); as large as the USA		

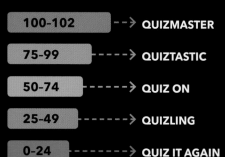

HOW WELL DID YOU DO?

100-102	--→ **QUIZMASTER**
75-99	----→ **QUIZTASTIC**
50-74	-----→ **QUIZ ON**
25-49	------→ **QUIZLING**
0-24	-------→ **QUIZ IT AGAIN**

GLOSSARY

algae A very simple type of plant, such as seaweed

ancestors Relatives who lived a long time ago

civilization An advanced society with its own culture

climate Weather conditions

continent One of the seven main areas of land on Earth

crust The outer layer of Earth

diverse Including many different types

empire A group of countries or regions that are ruled by one group

enclaved A country that is located entirely or mostly within another country

equator An imaginary line that goes around the center of Earth

evaporates Changes from a liquid to a gas or vapor

geology The study of the rocks that make up Earth's surface

glaciers Large masses of ice that move slowly

hemisphere One half of Earth

holy Important for religious reasons

Indigenous A collective name that describes the original inhabitants of a place

invertebrates Animals without a backbone, such as insects or shellfish

irrigates Waters land so that crops will grow on it

mammals Types of warm-blooded animals that usually give birth to live young

mantle The part of Earth that is under the crust

native Describes a plant or animal that lives naturally in a place and has not been brought from somewhere else

peak The top of a mountain

plateau A large flat area of land that is above sea level

population density The number of people who live in a specific area

river basin The area of land where water flows into a river

tectonic plates Sections of Earth's crust

treaty A written agreement between countries

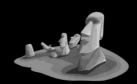

FURTHER INFORMATION

BOOKS

Reynolds, Toby. *Continents of the World*.
Crabtree Publishing, 2019.

Rockett, Paul. Mapping the Continents (series).
Crabtree Publishing, 2017.

The Seven Continents (series).
Children's Press, 2019.

WEBSITES

kids.nceas.ucsb.edu/biomes/desert.html
Explore desert habitats and the animals and plants that live there.

www.dkfindout.com/us/earth/continents
Learn more about the seven continents.

**https://kids.nationalgeographic.com/
explore/nature/habitats/ocean**
Discover some amazing facts about Earth's oceans.

INDEX